SEEDS SPROUT!

Mary Dodson Wade

Series Science Consultant:
Mary Poulson, Ph.D.
Associate Professor of Plant Biology
Department of Biological Sciences
Central Washington University
Ellensburg, WA

Series Literacy Consultant:
Allan A. De Fina, Ph.D.
Past President of the New Jersey Reading Association
Chairperson, Department of Literacy Education
New Jersey City University
Jersey City, NJ

CONTENTS

WORDS TO KNOW

protect (proh TEKT)—To keep something safe.

sprout (SPROWT)—To grow. When a seed begins to grow, it sprouts.

PARTS OF A PLANT

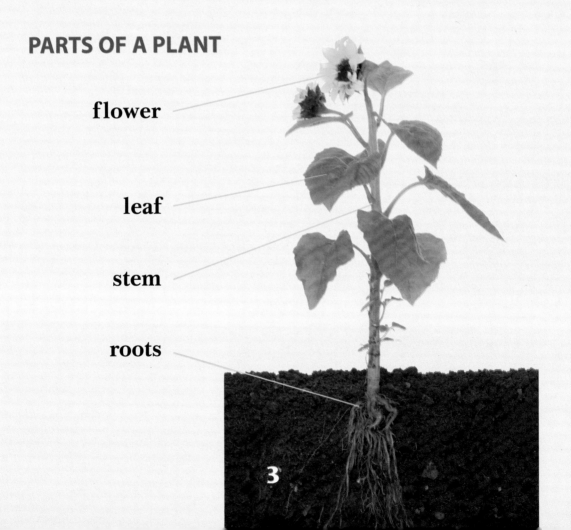

flower

leaf

stem

roots

3

The largest seed in the world is the sea coconut.

SEEDS—
BIG AND SMALL

Most plants make seeds. Some plants make big seeds. Some plants make tiny seeds. The largest seed in the world is the sea coconut. This seed weighs as much as a small child. Indian paintbrush flower seeds are as tiny as the sharp tip of a pencil.

Some seeds are very small, like these from a columbine plant.

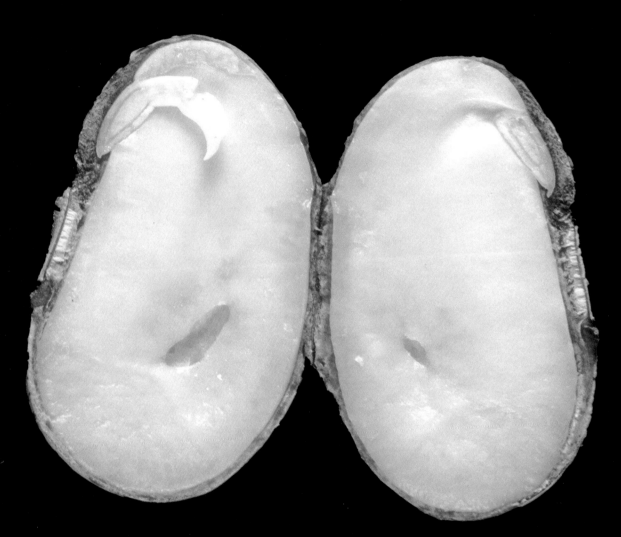

A seed has everything needed to make a new plant.

WHAT IS INSIDE A SEED?

Seeds are one way a plant makes more plants. Each seed has a baby plant inside it. It also has all the food the baby plant needs to start growing.

This seed has sprouted. It has started to grow.

WHAT IS A FRUIT?

A fruit is the part of a plant that holds the seeds. You know fruits such as peaches and apples, but beans and tomatoes are actually fruits too. The fruit carries the seeds to their new home. Fruits help spread seeds from one place to another.

A strawberry has many seeds.

8

An apple has a few seeds.

A coconut seed may travel in the water.
It sprouts on a beach.

HOW DO SEEDS TRAVEL?

Wind can blow seeds into the air. Some seeds travel by sticking to socks or animal fur. If the fruit floats, water can carry the seeds far away. Animals eat fruit and then leave the seeds behind in their droppings.

Dandelion seeds may be blown to new places.

HOW MANY SEEDS DO FRUITS HAVE?

A peach has only one seed inside.

Pea pods have a few seeds inside.

peach

pea pods

12

honeydew melons

honeydew melons

Some fruits have many seeds. Melons have too many seeds to count easily!

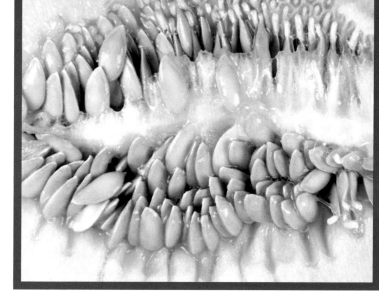

melon seeds

Acorns hold the seeds of an oak tree.

WHAT IS A SEED COAT?

A seed has a cover called a seed coat.

The seed coat **protects** the baby plant.

Tomato seeds have a soft coat.

Oak tree seeds have a hard coat.

HOW DOES A SEED
SPROUT?

The new plant cannot grow inside the seed coat. It must wait for the seed coat to open. Water can soften the seed coat. The soft seed coat splits. Then the new plant starts growing.

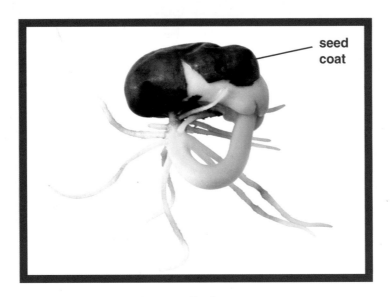

seed
coat

DO SEEDS MAKE NEW PLANTS?

Each seed can make
a new plant.

The new
plant grows
and grows.

◄ Someday it will look like the plant from which the seed came.

Then the plant ► will make more seeds to grow new plants.

seeds

19

DOES SOAKING A SEED MAKE IT SPROUT FASTER?

You will need:
* ✳ 4 bean seeds
* ✳ a cup of water
* ✳ 2 paper towels
* ✳ paper and pen

1. Place 2 bean seeds in a cup of warm water for one hour.

2. Remove the 2 bean seeds from the cup of water.

3. Place these seeds between the layers of a damp paper towel. Label these bean seeds "soaked."

4. Place the other 2 bean seeds between the layers of a damp paper towel. Label these bean seeds "not soaked."

5. Check your seeds every day. Keep the towels damp. Which seeds sprout first? Did soaking the seeds to soften the seed coat make a difference?

6. Try this experiment with different types of seeds. What do you find out?

LEARN MORE

BOOKS

Bodach, Vijaya Khisty. *Fruits*. Mankato, Minn.:
Capstone Press, 2007.

Fowler, Allan. *From Seed to Plant*. New York:
Children's Press, 2001.

Lobb, Janice. *Dig and Sow! How Do Plants Grow?*
New York: Kingfisher, 2000.

Stone, Lynn. *Seeds*. Vero Beach, Fla.: Rourke
Publishing, 2008.

LEARN MORE

WEB SITES

Globio. *Glossopedia*. **"Plants."**
   <http://www.globio.org/glossopedia/article.
   aspx?art_id=30>

University of Illinois. *The Great Plant Escape.*
   <http://www.urbanext.uiuc.edu/gpe>

U.S. Department of Agriculture. *Sci4Kids*. **"Plants."**
   <http://www.ars.usda.gov/is/kids/plants/
   plantsintro.htm>

INDEX

Enslow Elementary, an imprint of Enslow Publishers, Inc.
Enslow Elementary® is a registered trademark of
Enslow Publishers, Inc.

Copyright © 2009 by Enslow Publishers, Inc.

Library of Congress Cataloging-in-Publication Data

Wade, Mary Dodson.
  Seeds sprout! / by Mary Dodson Wade.
   p. cm. — (I like plants!)
  Summary: "Presents information about seeds, including
where they come from, how they grow, and how they
travel"—Provided by publisher.
  Includes bibliographical references and index.
  ISBN-13: 978-0-7660-3154-8 (library ed.)
  ISBN-10: 0-7660-3154-3 (library ed.)
  1. Seeds—Juvenile literature. 2. Germination—Juvenile
literature. I. Title.
  QK661.W33 2009
  581.4'67—dc22   2007039461

ISBN-13: 978-0-7660-3614-7 (paperback)
ISBN-10: 0-7660-3614-6 (paperback)

Printed in the United States of America
062013 Bang Printing, Brainerd, Minn.
10 9 8 7 6 5 4 3

To Our Readers: We have done our best to make sure all
Internet Addresses in this book were active and appropriate
when we went to press. However, the author and the publisher
have no control over and assume no liability for the material
available on those Internet sites or on other Web sites they may
link to. Any comments or suggestions can be sent by e-mail to
comments@enslow.com or to the address on the back cover.

Every effort has been made to locate all copyright holders of
material used in this book. If any errors or omissions have occurred,
corrections will be made in future editions of this book.

♻ Enslow Publishers, Inc., is committed to printing our books on
recycled paper. The paper in every book contains 10% to 30% post-
consumer waste (PCW). The cover board on the outside of each book
contains 100% PCW. Our goal is to do our part to help young peo-
ple and the environment too!

Note to Parents and Teachers: The *I Like Plants!* series supports the
National Science Education Standards for K–4 science. The Words to
Know section introduces subject-specific vocabulary words, including
pronunciation and definitions. Early readers may need help with
these new words.

Photo Credits: © Chris Ridley/Alamy, p. 4; © Duncan Usher/Foto
Natura/Minden Pictures, p. 19 (right); iStockphoto.com: © Alina
Solovyova-Vincent, p. 20, © Malcolm Romain, p. 3, © Matej
Michelizza, p. 18 (right), © ushama, p. 1, © Viktor Kitaykin, p. 16;
Photo Researchers, Inc.: F. Stuart Westmorland, p. 10, Herman
Eisenbeiss, p. 14, Perennou Nuridsany, p. 11; Shutterstock, pp. 2, 7,
9, 12 (peach and peas), 13 (melon seeds), 15, 19 (left), 23; Visuals
Unlimited: © David Cavagnaro, p. 4 (inset), © Dr. Robert Calentine,
p. 22, © Howard Rice/Gap Photo, p. 5, © Inga Spence, pp. 8, 13
(melons), © Nigel Cattlin, pp. 6, 17, 18 (left), © Ray Coleman, p. 14
(inset).

Cover Photo: © Nigel Cattlin/Visuals Unlimited

Enslow Elementary
an imprint of
Enslow Publishers, Inc.
40 Industrial Road
Box 398
Berkeley Heights, NJ 07922
USA
http://www.enslow.com